HISTORY THROUGH SOURCES

The Rise of Islam

RIGBY INTERACTIVE LIBRARY

Richard Tames

RIGBY
INTERACTIVE
LIBRARY

This edition © 1996 Rigby Education
Published by Rigby Interactive Library,
an imprint of Rigby Education,
division of Reed Elsevier, Inc.
500 Coventry Lane,
Crystal Lake, IL 60014

Text © Richard Tames 1996

Printed in Hong Kong

00 99 98 97 96
10 9 8 7 6 5 4 3 2 1

Library of Congress Cataloging-in-Publication Data
Tames, Richard.
   The rise of Islam/Richard Tames.
      p. cm. — (History through sources—Rigby
      Interactive library)
   Includes bibliographical references and index.
   Summary: Covers the history of the Muslim
religion from its founding by Muhammad through its
spread among Arabs and other peoples.
   ISBN 1-57572-010-8 (lib. bdg.)
   1. Islam—History—Juvenile literature. [1. Islam—
History.]   I. Title.   II. Series.
BP50.T27 1996
297'.09—dc20   95-20616
                                                       CIP
                                                        AC

Designed by Ron Kamen, Green Door Design

Produced by AMR

Illustrated by Jeff Edwards

Acknowledgments

The author and publisher would like to thank the
following for permission to reproduce photographs:

A. C. Cooper Ltd: p.7, p.20, p.27
Ancient Art & Architecture Collection: p.5, p.11, p.38
Bodleian Library, Oxford: p.30
British Museum/Robert Harding Picture Library: p.31
Giraudon Paris: p.36
Peter Sanders: p.4
Robert Harding Picture Library: p.25
Roland & Sabrina Michaud/John Hilielson Agency: p.26
Sonia Halliday Photographs: p.13, p.14, p.24, p.37
University of Oxford Museum of the History of Science:
p.19
Victoria & Albert Museum: p.41

Cover photograph reproduced with permission of Sonia
Halliday Photographs

The author and publisher would also like to thank
Dr. M. Ahsan of the Islamic Foundation for his
comments in the preparation of this book.

Every effort has been made to contact copyright holders
of any material reproduced in this book. Any omissions
will be rectified in subsequent printings if notice is given
to the publisher.

Details of Written Sources

Sources in this book are both primary and secondary.
Primary sources are texts, eyewitness accounts, quotations,
photographs, or artwork that date from the historical period.
Secondary sources are analyses by experts in the field. In
some cases, the wording and sentence structure of sources
have been simplified to ensure that they are accessible to
students.

Akbar S. Ahmed, *Discovering Islam*, Routledge, 1988: 1.2, 2.3
T. W. Arnold, *The Preaching of Islam*, Luzac & Co., 1986: 3.8
A. S. Beveridge (trans.), *The Baburnama*, Luzac & Co., 1921: 5.5
Claude Cahen in P. M. Holt, A. K. S. Lambton & B. Lewis
(eds.), *The Cambridge History of Islam*, Vol. 2, Cambridge
University Press, 1970: 3.1
K. N. Chaudhurie, *Asia Before Europe*, Cambridge University
Press, 1990: 3.9
Riadh El-Droubie, *Islamic Correspondence Course*, Minaret
House, n.d.: 1.4
Richard Ettinghausen in B. Lewis (ed.), *The World of Islam*,
Thames & Hudson, 1976: 3.13
E. S. Forster (trans.), *The Turkish Letters of Ogier Ghiselin de
Busbecq*, Clarendon Press, 1927: 3.15, 5.3, 5.4
Sir Hamilton Gibb (trans.), *Ibn Battuta: Travels in Asia and
Africa*, Routledge & Kegan Paul, 1929: 4.1, 4.3, 4.4, 4.5
D. G. E. Hall, *A History of South-East Asia*, Hodder &
Stoughton, 1954: 4.2
Philip K. Hitti, *Capital Cities of Arab Islam*, Cornell
University Press, 1973: 2.5
Chris Horris and Peter Chippendale, *What Is Islam?*,
W. H. Allen, 1990: 1.3, 2.6
Hugh Kennedy, *The Prophet and the Age of the Caliphates*,
Longman, 1986: 2.7
Bernard Lewis, *Istanbul and the Civilisation of the Ottoman
Empire*, University of Oklahoma Press, 1963: 5.1, 5.2
Bernard Lewis, *Islam: From the Prophet Muhammad to the
Capture of Constantinople*, Harper & Row, 1974: 2.1, 2.2, 3.11,
3.14
Raphaela Lewis, *Everyday Life in Ottoman Turkey*, Batsford,
1971: 3.10
Maurice Lombard, *The Golden Age of Islam*, Elsevier, 1975:
3.12
W. H. McNeil and M. R. Waldmann, *The Islamic World*,
Oxford University Press, 1973: 5.6, 5.7
Harold Osborne (ed.), *Oxford Companion to the Decorative
Arts*, Oxford University Press, 1975: 2.4
Xavier de Planhol, *The Islamic World: An Essay in Religious
Geography*, Cornell University Press, 1957: 3.2
Malise Ruthven, *Islam in the World*, Penguin, 1984: 6.1
W. M. Watt: *A History of Islamic Spain*, Edinburgh University
Press, 1965: 3.7

Note to the Reader

In this book some words are printed in **bold** type. This
indicates that the word is listed in the glossary on
pages 46–47. The glossary gives a brief explanation of
words that may be new to you.

Contents

The Religion of Islam

Muhammad: The Man and His Message

Islam is sometimes called "the youngest of the world religions," but Muslims believe there has only ever been one true religion—to worship and obey Allah, the only God. Allah has sent **prophets** to teach people this ever since He created the world. However, humans have either failed to listen, to understand, or to remember. Islam, like Christianity and **Judaism**, is part of a shared religious tradition stretching back to the prophet Abraham. Muslims believe that Muhammad's mission was to bring that tradition of teaching to its final and perfect end.

The flag of Saudi Arabia bears the Muslim declaration of faith: "There is no god but Allah, and Muhammad is His Prophet."

Muhammad's Achievement

Muhammad (570–632) was born in Arabia, where **idol** worship was the main religion and tribes were always fighting each other. His teaching and example converted the Arabs into a united nation of believers in Allah. Within one century of his death the Arabs had conquered an immense realm, where Arabic became the common language and the laws of Islam were obeyed. Although this realm broke up, the Islamic world was still held together by religion, trade, law, and language, and Islam continued to spread throughout the world making converts.

Success Is Not Enough

Muhammad was born into a noble but poor family in the trading city of Mecca. He trained as a merchant, traveled widely and won a reputation for honesty. At the age of 25 he married his employer, Khadija, a wealthy widow of 40, and could have lived easily for the rest of his life. However, he was upset by life in Mecca, where greed, **superstition**, and poverty were all too common. Muhammad often went into the deserts and hills to be alone and think deeply about life and how it should be lived.

Messages from God

When he was around 40 years old, Muhammad was in a cave on Mount Hira when he believed that God, through the Angel Gabriel, came to him with a message. Muhammad had these messages for the rest of his life, but only began to teach about them three years after they began, when he was sure that he was not just suffering from a mental illness. The messages came in the form of wonderful poetry. As the Arabs loved poetry, many people began to listen to Muhammad when he repeated them in public. After his death, they were collected together and written down to make the **Qur'an** ("Recitation"), the Holy Book of Islam.

For Muslims, the Qur'an is the most important book in the world and should be made a precious object of beauty.

Exile ...

Muhammad's teachings spoke out against the rich and powerful who cared only for themselves. He protested against the worship of useless idols, against gambling, drunkenness, and the neglect of widows and orphans. By 622, Muhammad was so unpopular with the people whom he criticized, that he had to leave Mecca with his followers. They accepted an invitation to Medina, an **oasis** whose people wanted Muhammad to be their judge. Muslims call this event the **hijra** ("departure"), because it marks the beginning of when Muslims first lived together according to the rules of Islam. It also became the starting point for the Islamic calendar.

... And Return

War broke out between Muhammad's followers and the people of Mecca. Meanwhile, more and more Arab tribes became Muslims. By 630, Muhammad was powerful enough to march on Mecca with an army so huge that the city surrendered almost without a fight. Muhammad then made a special point of clearing all the idols out of the Ka'ba, the city's most sacred shrine. In 632, Muhammad suddenly died. He had never claimed to be more than a man, but the Muslims were surprised.

SOURCE 1

It (the Qur'an) is no new tale of fiction, but confirms existing holy books, explains all things, and is a guidance and mercy for believers.

This source is taken from the Qur'an, Chapter 12, Verse 111.

SOURCE 2

In a short span he (Muhammad) had played the role of father, husband, chief, warrior, friend, and Prophet. For Muslims, the life of the Prophet is the triumph of hope over despair, light over darkness.

*From **Discovering Islam** by Akbar S. Ahmed, 1988.*

Islam: Belief and Behavior

Islam requires its followers not just to hold certain beliefs but also to obey detailed rules of behavior. There are five basic duties for a Muslim.

- **Shahadah** The statement of faith—to say and believe that: "There is no god but Allah (God) and Muhammad is His Messenger."
- **Salat** Prayers—said in Arabic, facing towards Mecca, five times a day.
- **Zakat** Charity—paying a donation of personal wealth, used to help the poor and for public benefits, like supporting colleges or hospitals.
- **Saum** Fasting—going completely without food or drink, from dawn to sunset throughout Ramadan, the month when Muhammad first began to receive **revelations** from God.
- **Hajj** Pilgrimage—visiting Mecca, where Islam was first preached, at least once in a lifetime; but only if it is possible to afford it and not endanger one's family.

Islamic Law

The Qur'an lays down rules for such basic matters as prayer and pilgrimage, marriage and divorce, inheritance and warfare. In the centuries after Muhammad's death, as the Islamic realm expanded and new circumstances arose, learned judges (**ulama**) tried to develop rules for every possible situation. They believed that laws came from God, not humans. If they could not find an answer in the Qur'an, they studied what Muhammad had said or done. Gradually, they built up a huge body of learning which divided every action into one of five categories— forbidden, discouraged, neutral, encouraged and compulsory. All Islamic governments were supposed to uphold these laws.

The Sufi Way

Apart from the judges, a very different kind of holy person developed in Islam. They were called **Sufis** because they wore simple, rough robes (suf). They believed that the way to find God was not through rules but by looking inside yourself. They had different ways of doing this: through chanting, dancing, breathing exercises, or fasting. Some wrote poetry in praise of God or describing their experiences. Ordinary people believed that many Sufis had magic powers or were able to heal the sick. Often, their tombs became places of pilgrimage.

A qadi (judge) applying Islamic law to settle a dispute between a man and his wives. Islam allows a man to have up to four wives, but this has been rare.

A wandering Sufi master surrounded by his devoted followers.

The spirit of Hajj is the spirit of total sacrifice—of comforts, pleasures, wealth, companionship, vanities of dress, and pride relating to birth, nation, work, or status. Hajj also signifies the brotherhood of all Muslims, demonstrated in this greatest of all international assemblies. It reminds Muslims of the future assembly on the Day of Judgment and also of the birth, rise and expansion of Islam, the establishment of the worship of one God and the hardships of the Prophet Muhammad (peace be on him) and the early Muslims.

A quote from Hajji Riadh El-Droubie, an Iraqi living in London, 1970.

AL-GHAZALI

Al-Ghazali (1058–1111) was one of the few people ever to be taught both Islamic law and to be a Sufi. He had a brilliant career as a teacher and then had a breakdown which left him mentally disabled. He gave up all his wealth and lived as a poor wanderer for ten years. Then he spent the rest of his life explaining how the rules of Islam could be lived to help a Muslim find the true path to knowing God.

SOURCE **3**

Unlike Christianity, Islam could never become a private religion. Rather it is a complete way of life governing dress, business, taxation, justice and punishment, politics, war and peace, family life, the care of animals, education, diet, forms of greeting, and rules of hospitality. Even the way in which a glass of water is to be drunk is governed by Islamic religious law.

*From **What is Islam?** by Chris Horris and Peter Chippindale, 1990.*

Caliphs, Conquests, and Conversions

Companions and Conquests

The generation after Muhammad's death saw Islam expand through conquest and split over power.

When Muhammad died, the Muslims chose one of his oldest friends, Abu Bakr, to be their leader. He was known as the Khalifa (or Caliph, which means successor). Some Arab tribes broke away from Islam because they thought they only had to be loyal to Muhammad, not the religion. Abu Bakr sent Muslim armies to punish them. Their campaigns soon turned into a general war which expanded Muslim territory, as tribes brought back to loyalty turned on neighboring tribes, until a clash with the great empires of Byzantium and Persia (present day Iran) was bound to happen.

The Early Conquests

The Muslim armies, although poorly armed, soon conquered the rich provinces of Syria and Egypt from Byzantium, and overthrew the Persian empire entirely. Their astonishing success can be explained by the following reasons:

- Byzantium and Persia had been fighting each other for more than 20 years and were exhausted.
- The Arabs were superb light cavalry and well experienced at hit-and-run tactics which the slow-moving armies of their enemies found hard to deal with.
- The Arabs had previously used all their energy to fight each other and had never before been united as a single force.

This map shows the expansion of Islam during the lifetime of the Prophet and the first four caliphs.

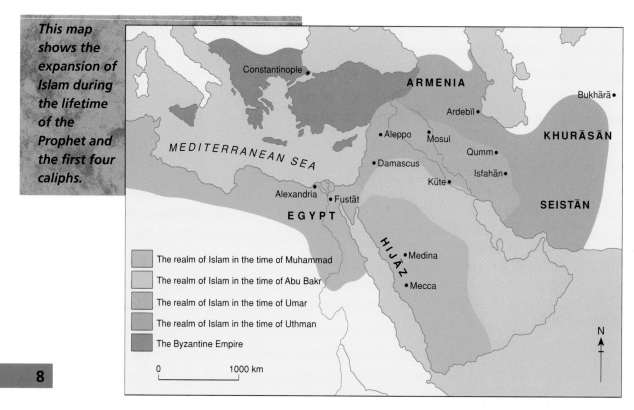

The realm of Islam in the time of Muhammad

The realm of Islam in the time of Abu Bakr

The realm of Islam in the time of Umar

The realm of Islam in the time of Uthman

The Byzantine Empire

0   1000 km

- The Muslim armies learned new military skills from their defeated enemies, such as how to build machines to throw rocks at city walls or how to fight at sea in ships.
- The Byzantines had made many cities pay heavy taxes, and treated their people badly, because their Christian beliefs were not exactly the same as the Byzantines—often, the Muslims were welcomed as **liberators**.
- Islam gave its followers discipline and the belief that, if they were killed fighting for their religion, they would go straight to heaven.

Companions of the Prophet

Abu Bakr died two years after becoming leader and was succeeded by Umar and then Uthman. All of them had known Muhammad personally. Muslims readily accepted their orders because of their just, democratic, and pious rule and because they knew Muhammad. They became known as the **Rashidun**—"rightly-guided Caliphs."

Islam Divided

After Uthman's death in 656, Ali, the son-in-law of Muhammad, became Caliph. But his position was challenged by Mu'awiyah, nephew of Uthman and a leader of the powerful Umayyad family, which had once persecuted the early Muslims. Mu'awiyah controlled the rich province of Syria. Ali was murdered. Later, his son, Hussain, was killed, and his other son, Hasan, was forced to step aside. This quarrel over who should be caliph split Islam between those who thought it should be Ali and his family because they were related to Muhammad, and those who did not. The former became known as Shi'ites, the latter as Sunnis. Shi'ites make up about 10 to 15 percent of all Muslims today, but Iran is the only wholly Shi'ite country.

SOURCE 1

In the name of God, the Merciful, the Compassionate. Become Muslims and be saved. If not, accept our protection and pay taxes to us. Or else I shall come against you with men who love death as you love to drink wine.

Khalid Ibn Al-Walid challenges the border chiefs of the Persian Realm in 636. From **Islam: From the Prophet Muhammad to the Capture of Constantinople** *by Bernard Lewis, 1974.*

SOURCE 2

You had only cane lances, tipped with ox-horn, and used to ride bareback. You used to fight in unruly bands. You used not to fight at night and knew nothing about ambush. Nor did you know anything of the machines of war—the battering ram, the catapult or how to throw fire.

Writer Al-Jahiz, records the disbelief of Persians who were defeated by Muslims, fighting only with feeble cane lances, around 800.

KHALID IBN AL-WALID

Khalid Ibn Al-Walid (died 642) at first fought against Muhammad and only became a Muslim in 629. He became one of the greatest Muslim generals, capturing Damascus and smashing a vast Byzantine army at the Yarmuk River in 636, where 50,000 Byzantine troops were slaughtered. Khalid was known as Sayf Allah—Sword of God.

The First Realm

The Umayyads tried to change a series of conquered provinces into a true realm—and hold it by force.

Mu'awiyah, the founder of the Umayyad **Dynasty**, moved the capital of his realm to Damascus, a beautiful and ancient city in Syria. Here, he and his successors lived in great luxury, remote from ordinary people. This was different from the first four caliphs who had lived simply, just as leaders of Arab tribes had always done. The Umayyad caliphs were surrounded by officials and bodyguards. Rebels against their rule were brutally crushed.

Meanwhile, conquering Muslim armies spread the frontiers of their Realm as far west as Spain and as far east as the borders of India and China. As long as the expansion went on fast enough, ambitious leaders who failed to win rewards in Damascus could succeed on the new frontiers. But when expansion finally slowed, the system broke down.

Changes in Government

During the first phase of Arab conquests, daily life for the people changed very little, apart from those who actually ruled and lived off the taxes. Local Byzantine and Persian officials kept their jobs and used Greek and Persian to write letters and record taxes. The conquering Arab armies lived apart in garrison cities.

Under the Umayyads this changed. They were Arab **aristocrats** and they favored other Arabs and other aristocrats. Even Christians and Jews were given positions of power, providing they were Arabs. Arabic became the official language of government. A new Arabic coinage replaced old imitations of Byzantine and Persian coins. Because the only way most people ever saw their ruler was as a picture on a coin, this was a powerful way of telling them who was in charge. A new postal service was set up between Damascus and the capitals of each province so that the Umayyad government could keep up with events.

This map shows the Umayyad Realm at its greatest extent.

Britain

EUROPE

Spain
Cordoba

Greece

Turkey

Syria

MEDITERRANEAN SEA

Damascus • Baghdad   Persia

Morocco

Cairo •

Egypt

Arabia
• Medina

AFRICA

• Mecca   The birthplace
of Muhammad

N

Muslim lands
Byzantine Empire

0   1600 km

A silver dirham minted by the Umayyads, showing the governor of a conquered territory. Notice the inscription in Arabic.

Decline and Disaster

In 717, a Muslim army was badly defeated by the Byzantines. Then, an unusually fair-minded caliph, Umar II (reigned 717–720) tried to soothe non-Arab Muslim converts by giving them the same pay and tax rights as Arab Muslims. This wrecked the government's finances. Quarrels between different Arab tribes over the best jobs weakened the army. Hisham (reigned 724–743) was strong enough to regain control while he lived, but after his reign, the Arab tribes began to fight each other again.

Al-Walid II (reigned 743–744) was a drunken wastrel who spent such huge sums of money that his own family had him murdered. He was followed in quick succession by three more caliphs. Seeing how Arab power was weakening, non-Arab Greek and Persian converts began to support a secret revolutionary organization against Umayyad rule. In 750, they rose in revolt. Umayyad rule ended in bloodshed.

SOURCE 3

The Abbasid general Abdillah invited eighty leading Umayyads to dinner on a hot night in June 750. When the guests sat down to eat, they were attacked by soldiers. After the slaughter of the Umayyads servants spread carpets on their squirming, dying bodies and the guests continued to eat and make merry. Even the dead and buried were not spared. Tombs of Umayyad caliphs were ransacked. Only that of the pious Umar II was spared. The youthful Abdur–Rahman, a grandson of the tenth Umayyad caliph, escaped to Spain to establish a glorious dynasty there.

*From **Discovering Islam** by Akbar S.Ahmed, 1988.*

SOURCE 4

It would be wrong to imagine that the fall of the dynasty was inevitable. The Umayyad regime had never been as strong as it had been under Hisham only a decade before the final collapse. It was only the failure of leadership and murderous conflicts that followed his death that led to disaster.

*From **The Prophet and the Age of the Caliphates** by Hugh Kennedy, 1986.*

The Abbasid Realm

Between 750 and 1258, the Islamic world was ruled as a single great realm—at least in theory.

The second Abbasid caliph, Al-Mansur (reigned 754–775) used the captured treasury of the Umayyads to build a new capital at Baghdad in Iraq. 100,000 men slaved to build a circular city, with walls 99 feet high and 43 feet wide at the top. Work began in 758, and four years later the Caliph moved in. The city continued to expand until it had a population of over 1 million and was probably the biggest city in the world—except, perhaps, for Xi'an in China.

Baghdad became the Islamic world's greatest center of power, wealth, and learning. The move to Baghdad shifted the heart of Islam eastward and increased the influence of Persians rather than Arabs at court. Persian officials and soldiers became powerful. Their tastes in art, fashion, and even food became more influential.

A Golden Age

During the ninth century, Christian Europe was torn by war and raided by savage Vikings. There was little trade and few towns. The Islamic world by contrast was at the height of its power and prosperity. Muslims learned from Chinese prisoners-of-war the secret of making paper. Because paper was much cheaper than **papyrus** or **parchment** this helped everyone whose work involved writing, such as officials, scholars, and merchants.

The House of Wisdom

The Caliph Al-Mamun (reigned 813–833) gathered together the finest scholars and built a "House of Wisdom" in which they could work. Here ancient books from Greece, India, Persia and other countries could be kept safe and translated from their original languages into Arabic. In this way these books could be read from one end of the Islamic world to the other.

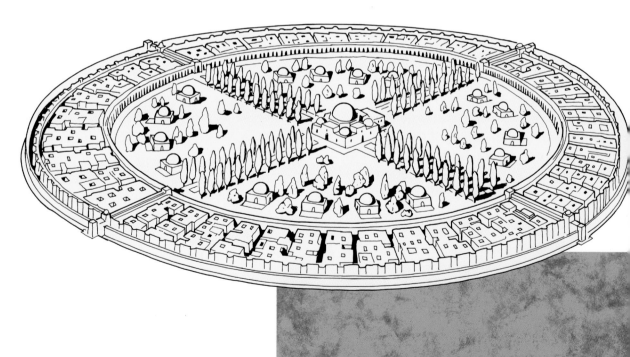

This is an artist's reconstruction of what the original circular city of Baghdad may have looked like.

Decline...

After the reign of Mutawakkil (reigned 847–861), the officials and generals who served the caliph became more powerful than the ruler himself. Sometimes, they even murdered the caliph and put another in his place. From 936 onwards, the top general often put his own name on coins alongside that of the caliph, to show that he was just as important. Distant provinces such as Spain, Morocco, Yemen, and Oman ignored the orders of Baghdad and came under the control of local rulers.

... And Fall

Abbasid rule was finally finished off by Mongol invaders from the east. They destroyed the great Muslim trading cities on the "Silk Road" to the east, such as Samarkand and Bokhara. Then they sacked Baghdad itself, killing the last Abbasid caliph. In 1401, another Mongol, Tamerlane, destroyed what little they had left. After the destruction of Baghdad, Cairo became the greatest city in the Muslim world.

The Mongols under Hulagu lay siege to Baghdad in 1258. This picture was painted in Persia about 200 years later.

SOURCE 5

The events of 1258 were a calamity for Islam, the Persian nation, and the whole of mankind. Human culture was set back at least a century by the destruction of centers of learning and the murder of hundreds of scholars and scientists. The Mongol destruction of the Abbasid Realm also brought an end to the dream of maintaining a unified Islamic Empire.

*From **What is Islam?** by Chris Horrie and Peter Chippindale, 1990.*

HUNAYN IBN ISHAQ

Hunayan Ibn Ishaq (808–873) was a Christian appointed by Al-Mamun to be head of the "House of Wisdom". Under Al-Mutawakkil he also became chief physician of the court. He traveled through Syria and Egypt, gathering ancient manuscripts. Without the translations he made, most of the writings of the great Greek doctor, Galen, would have been lost for ever. The Caliph was so grateful that for every book by Galen translated, he was paid its weight in gold. Hunayan also wrote the first textbook about eye diseases.

Challenge and Recovery: The Crusades

The wars known as Crusades led to closer contact between the Muslim and Christian worlds and had a deep effect on European lifestyles.

Jerusalem and other Christian holy places came under Muslim control in the seventh century. But, Christian pilgrims were allowed to visit them in peace until the 11th century, when the area was taken over by Seljuq Turks. They had only recently become Muslims and were **intolerant** toward other religions. They also threatened the weak Christian empire of Byzantium.

The Byzantine emperor asked the Pope to send him some volunteer soldiers as reinforcements for his army. The Pope's appeal was so successful, however, that a huge independent European army set out to reconquer the Holy Land from Muslim control. The invaders wore the sign of the Cross as their badge and were known as Crusaders ("crux" means "cross" in Latin).

Both Byzantines and Muslims thought the Crusaders were dirty, crude, and brutal, but also tough and brave. After going through terrible hardships, the Crusaders took Jerusalem by storm in 1099 and celebrated by murdering its people—Muslims, Jews, and Christians alike. Because the leaders of the Crusade each wanted land for themselves, they set up four small kingdoms in the surrounding area—which were bound to be weaker than one single Christian state.

A 14th century French artist's idea of what the Crusaders' attack on Jerusalem might have looked like.

The Counterattack

The success of the first Crusade came about because the local Muslim leaders were too busy quarreling with each other to fight the invaders. As they reunited under a succession of able leaders such as Zangi, Saladin, and Baybars, they gradually conquered back the Christian territories. Six more major Crusades set out from the West, but none was able to do more than win small and temporary successes. The last Christian stronghold, the port of Acre, fell in 1291.

What the Crusades Did for Europe

The Crusades made a far deeper impact on Europe than on the Middle East. The idea of fighting for the Christian faith led to the reconquest of Spain from Muslim control and the conquest of much of eastern Europe from pagan rule. It also inspired much poetry and art, which portrayed the Crusader as a brave, unselfish hero.

Warfare itself changed as a result of the Crusading experience, leading to improvements in castle-building and siege-craft. Contact with Eastern lifestyles gave Europe's upper classes a taste for new luxuries such as fine textiles, spices, sugar, perfumes, mirrors, carpets, paper, and even bathing to keep clean. Chess and new kinds of music became popular. Fashion, diet, leisure, and trade were all, therefore, greatly affected by the Crusades.

SOURCE 6

New fabrics, new designs, and an interest in hairdressing were the first noticeable signs that a change in traditional costume had begun; and by about 1130 women's clothes had taken on a completely new silhouette. The accent on the hair was as noticeable with the well-dressed man as with his wife. The 13th century continued in adapting the silhouette of the crusader. Basically this could be traced to the surcote or tabard, which had been originally devised to protect the armor both from the heat of the sun and from rusting during rainstorms. A particularly interesting headdress of the period can be traced to its inspiration from the Crusaders' chain-mail head covering.

From "Costume," The Oxford Companion to the Decorative Arts, 1975.

USAMAH IBN MUNQIDH

Usamah Ibn Munqidh was born in 1095, the year the First Crusade was organized, and lived to be more than 90 years old, when he wrote his memoirs. He was the nephew of a Syrian prince, fought as a warrior, and was a friend of Saladin. He thought newly arrived crusaders were very rude, but became more civilized the longer they stayed. Usamah also thought Western medicine crude and the Western method of settling legal disputes by duels or ordeals as quite barbaric.

Islam as a Way of Life

Cities

The Muslim world had far more and far larger cities than any country in medieval Europe.

In the early period of the Arab conquests, the Muslim armies built military camps, such as Kufa and Basra in Iraq, where they could live apart from the conquered peoples. Within 30 years of being founded, Kufa had 100,000 people and Basra 200,000. In 641, a camp was founded at Fustat by the Nile. In 969 a walled city, Cairo (or Al-Qahira, meaning "victorious") was built nearby. By 1340 Cairo had a population of 500,000—making it 10 times as big as London was at that time. Cairo's Al-Azhar University has been the leading center of Islamic learning for 1,000 years.

Cities Spread West

As the Muslims took control of North Africa, they founded great cities where none had existed before, such as Kairwan in Tunisia, Oran in Algeria, and Fez in Morocco. In Spain, they revived cities that had once been great when part of the Roman Empire, such as Seville, Cadiz, and Toledo. Cordoba became the greatest city in Muslim Spain. By the 10th century it had pavements and street-lighting—1,000 years before London did.

*Massive 13th century walls still protect Cairo's fortified **citadel**.*

Cities on the Silk Road

The trade route from China to the Middle East was known as the Silk Road, because silk was one of China's main exports. The route ran through mountains, deserts, and vast plains inhabited by fierce **nomad** tribes. Cities like Bukhara and Samarkand had ramparts of wood and earth 62 miles around to protect them and the villages and fields that supplied their food. Samarkand has had a very turbulent history and has been conquered many times. Around 900, it had a population of 500,000. Between 1720 and 1770 it was quite deserted because it had been sacked so many times. Nowadays it again has a population of 500,000.

Capital Choice

Many major Islamic cities have kept their importance. Damascus, Baghdad, Cairo, Tunis, and Algiers are still, respectively, the capitals of Syria, Iraq, Egypt, Tunisia, and Algeria. Although Ankara has been the capital of Turkey since 1924, Istanbul remains the larger city.

Learning and Knowledge: Medicine, Mathematics, and Magic

Muslim scholars studied every kind of subject, because they believed that each part of God's creation was connected to the rest.

SOURCE 1

In the Muslim world, as in the ancient world, but unlike medieval Western Europe, the whole of civilization was found in the town; it was only there that government, law, religion, and culture existed. The majority of the Arabs settled in towns, almost never in the country. And the local people were attracted to the towns by the courts, business activities, and official careers.

From **Cambridge History Of Islam, Vol. 2 by Claude Cahen, 1970.**

SOURCE 2

The Muslim town obeys a number of well-defined general rules. The mosque is the heart of the whole complex. In the immediate neighborhood one finds the **bazaar**, a commercial district, with its booths and rows of shops set up around the khans, combinations of hotels and warehouses. In this area, too, one finds the public baths. The seat of government is not at the center but on the outskirts, ready to defend itself against riots or raids. The Jewish quarter, to protect itself against mobs, shelters near the palace. Then come the residential areas; then the semi-rural districts, occupied by farm laborers and then the cemeteries. Finally come the pastures and fields.

From **The Islamic World: An Essay in Religious Geography by Xavier de Planhol, 1957.**

Medicine

Islamic medicine was based on the Greek theory that all things, including the human body, consisted of mixtures of earth, air, fire, and water. Disease resulted from a lack of balance between these four elements and could be cured by drugs, diet, sleep, massage, or exercise. Surgery was used only if all else failed.

The Persian Muslim, Al-Razi (Rhazes) (865–923), recognized that smallpox and measles were different diseases; although they looked similar, they needed to be treated differently. He also wrote books called *Why Even Good Doctors Can't Cure All Diseases* and *Why Patients Prefer Lying Cheats to Good Doctors*.

The Spanish-born Abul-Qasem (Abulcasis) (936–1013) wrote an illustrated textbook of surgery, showing 200 instruments. It was translated into Latin by Gerard of Cremona (1114–1187) and used by European surgeons for the next 500 years.

SOURCE 3

They ask thee (Muhammad) concerning the new moons. Say: they are but signs to mark fixed periods of time in the affairs of men.

Unlike the Western calendar, the Islamic calendar is based on the lunar cycle. Here, the Qu'ran explains that the universe was organized so that humans could mark the passage of time by the regular appearance of the moon each month. Taken from the Qu'ran, Chapter IX, Verse 36.

Mathematics

Algebra and the use of decimals were developed by a Persian named Al-Khwarizmi (died about 850). The word "algebra" and other mathematical terms such as "zenith", and "nadir" all come from Arabic.

The numbers used in modern mathematics (1, 2, 3, 4, etc.) are usually called "Arabic numerals" to distinguish them from Roman numerals (I, II, III, IV, etc.). In fact, they were invented in India, but Europeans learned about them from Muslims.

Muslims used mathematics for practical jobs such as figuring out the times and direction of prayer and for surveying land. They also loved mathematical puzzles, like the "magic square" shown below. It uses the numbers 1 through 16 without repeating any of the numbers, and adds up to 34 whether they are added across, down, or diagonally:

15	10	3	6
4	5	16	9
14	11	2	7
1	8	13	12

Now try adding any group of two squares next to each other. What answer do you get?

SOURCE 4

It is God Who has set the stars for you that by them you might be guided in the shadows of land and sea.

Taken from the Qur'an, Chapter VI, Verse 97.

Science and Magic

Muslim scholars were fascinated by the stars and used **astronomy** to work out their calendar and how to navigate without landmarks, at sea or in the desert. Like Christians in medieval Europe, they also believed in **astrology**—that the movements of the stars and planets could be read to foretell events or lucky and unlucky days.

Both Muslims and Christians also practiced **alchemy**—experiments with chemistry to try to turn lead into gold or make a medicine that would help people live for ever. These experiments led to accidental discoveries that were often useful in dyeing cloth, glazing pottery, or working metal.

IBN SINA

Ibn Sina (980–1037), known in Europe as Avicenna, was a Persian doctor who wrote more than 200 books on subjects from music to mathematics. At the age of 10 he had memorized the whole Qur'an; by 16 he knew more than his teachers; by 21 years old he was a royal physician. His exciting life had times of wealth and power, and disgrace and imprisonment. His one-million word encyclopedia—*Canon of Medicine*—has been called the most important single book in the history of healing. In 16th century Europe it was printed no less than 36 times.

SOURCE 5

The **astrolabe** was a Greek invention, perfected by Muslims and used to take readings of the movements of the stars. It was used in navigation, surveying, making calendars, and teaching astronomy.

An astrolabe made in Toledo, Spain, and dated 1068. It was used by astronomers and sailors for marking the position of stars and planets.

Belief and Behavior: Christians and Jews

Muslims were usually willing to respect other religions and did not force conquered peoples to believe in Islam.

In many areas Muslim armies were welcomed. Usually, Arab commanders gave cities the chance to surrender in return for promises that the people's lives and houses would be safe, and that they would be allowed to keep their religion in peace. In return they would have to give up the right to carry weapons. In this way, the Muslims prevented much bloodshed.

Many Greeks and Persians converted to Islam and rose to high positions in the government. But Muslim rulers realized that it was also to their advantage for some of their subjects to remain Christians or Jews—because Muslims paid fewer taxes.

Protected Peoples

Muslims respected Christians and Jews as "Ahl Al-Kitab"—"People of the Book"—because they had written **scriptures**, the Bible, and the **Torah**. In Muslim lands they were allowed to live as **dhimmi**—protected peoples. They could only build new churches or **synagogues** after asking permission, and were not allowed to **convert** others to their faith. Often they had to wear special clothing so that they could be instantly recognized. Usually, they lived together in particular districts of a city.

Muslims, Jews and Christians shared a common heritage of stories found in the Old Testament of the Bible. This Muslim picture shows Moses (in Arabic, Musa) watching the Egyptian Pharaoh's army drowning in the Red Sea.

The **tolerant** policy of the Ottoman Realm (see page 35) attracted many non-Muslims who were being **persecuted** in Christian countries because of their beliefs—Protestants from Hungary and Silesia, Jews from Spain, and Cossacks from Russia.

SOURCE 6

Our Christian young men are drunk with the Arabic language and know nothing of the beauty of the Church's literature. They are so ignorant of their own language that there is hardly one in a thousand who can write a decent letter asking after a friend's health, while you can find a countless rabble who can learnedly churn out the grand-sounding rhythms of the Arab tongue. They can even make up poems in which every line ends with the same letter.

From the writings of an anonymous Christian writer in Spain, in 854.

SOURCE 7

One of the first steps taken by Muhammad II after the capture of Constantinople was to secure the allegiance of the Christians by proclaiming himself the protector of the Greek Church. Persecution of the Christians was strictly forbidden. Gennadios, the first patriarch after the Turkish conquest, received from the hands of the Sultan himself the pastoral staff, which was the sign of his office, together with a purse of 1,000 golden ducats and a horse with gorgeous trappings. The patriarch's court sat to decide all cases between Greeks. It could impose fines, imprison offenders in a prison provided for its own special use, and in some cases even condemn to capital punishment; while the ministers and officials of the government were directed to enforce its judgments.

*From **The Preaching of Islam** by T. W. Arnold, a British scholar, 1896.*

MOSES MAIMONIDES

Moses Maimonides (1134–1204) was one of the most skilled doctors of his time and also a great expert on Jewish law and religion. He was born into a wealthy and cultured Jewish family in Cordoba, Spain. At 13 he was forced to pretend to be a Muslim when the city was taken over by an extreme sect, the Almohads, who ended the usual policy of religious toleration. In 1159 Maimonides and his family fled to Fez in Morocco and later to Cairo. Shortly after their arrival, Maimonides's father died and his brother, a gem-dealer, drowned at sea, losing the family's entire fortune. To support his family Maimonides became physician to the local ruler and a lecturer at the state hospital. All through his troubled life he continued to write in both Arabic and Hebrew. His wisdom was respected by Jews, Christians and Muslims alike.

Work and Wealth: Crops, Herds and Crafts

For the first 1,000 years of its existence, the rulers and city-dwellers of the Muslim world enjoyed a much higher standard of living than the rulers and townspeople of Europe.

Crops

Although some Muslim regions, like the river valleys of Egypt and Iraq, were naturally fertile, most had very low rainfall. Muslim farmers therefore became experts at **irrigation**. They would cut canals, tanks and underground tunnels to catch, store, and distribute precious water. Thanks to their skill, crops such as rice, sugarcane, oranges and cotton spread through the dry Middle East and Mediterranean.

Farmers grew food for humans and fodder for animals. They also supplied vital raw materials for industry—cotton, wool, and silk for textiles; leather for boots, harness, and book bindings; wax, oils, and fats for soap, perfumes, and candles; indigo and saffron for dyeing cloth; flax for linen and paper.

Men tending medicinal herbs. The ones at the bottom left have a sieve and a rake. Another man is bringing a pitcher of cool water and a tray with bowls of olives for lunch.

Animals

Desert nomads, who drove their herds from one oasis to another, gathered dates and raised camels, sheep, and goats. Camels were used for long-distance transport. Sheep and goats provided fleece to be woven into cloth, and milk for cheese. Because Muslims are forbidden to eat pork, they relied on sheep and goats for most of their meat. Both of these animals grazed the land very closely. This meant that over the centuries many forest areas were destroyed, because the young shoots of trees and shrubs were eaten before they could grow. The Middle East was once much greener than it is today.

The Arabs delighted in breeding the finest horses. Only wealthy people could afford to use them for riding, racing, hunting, and war. Many poems were written to praise the best horses and riders. Donkeys were used for local transport and also to power waterwheels. Water-wheels were used in irrigation and the mills that pressed oil from olives.

Crafts

In major cities there were whole districts of craftsmen, usually making goods for the ruler and his court. Some cities specialized in particular goods. Damascus in Syria and Toledo in Spain were famed for steel swords; Fez in Morocco for leather goods; Samarkand in Central Asia for paper; Alexandria in Egypt for glass; and Isfahan and Tabriz in Persia for carpets.

SOURCE 8

A large proportion of crops raised in Iran, Afghanistan, and Oman was watered by underground channels running more than twenty miles in length. A regular line of stately plane trees seen near an Iranian village almost always shows that the underground channel has come to the surface and is flowing as an open stream. The trees were planted to protect the banks and reduce evaporation through their shade.

*From **Asia Before Europe** by K. N. Chaudhuri, 1990.*

SOURCE 9

The principal industries of the empire were primarily concerned with the production of war materials; at Samakar, a small town south of Sofia, alone, there were 17 iron factories making spades, anchors, horseshoes, nails, and similar products for the armed forces. A large part of the textile industry was engaged in making tent-cloths, ropes, and sails, in addition to cloth for uniforms; work in fur and skins, which included saddle and shoemaking, was also largely for military purposes.

*From **Everyday Life in Ottoman Turkey** by Raphaela Lewis, 1971.*

Work and Wealth: Trade

Even after the Islamic world broke up into many warring states, it was held together by long-distance trade.

The work of the merchant was greatly respected in Islam, because Muhammad himself had been one. The Middle East as a region was a natural market-place, lying at the junction of Asia, Africa, and Europe and of the Persian Gulf, Red Sea, Mediterranean Sea, and Black Sea. Trade was also helped by the fact that from one end of the Islamic world to the other Arabic was understood and the same laws were obeyed.

A marketplace in Yemen, depicted by a Syrian artist in 1237. In the background a trader is checking the weight of some coins to make sure they are genuine.

This map shows how the Islamic world drew on surrounding regions for its long-distance trade.

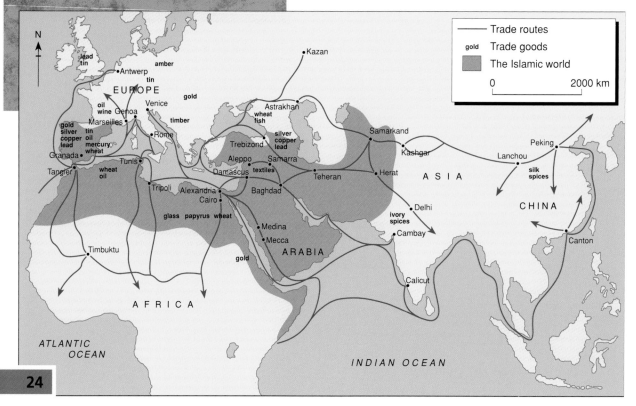

Mosques and Palaces

The Arabs originally lived in tents or simple homes made of mud brick. As they conquered different territories, they created a brilliant new style of architecture.

The early Arab conquerors used Byzantine and Persian craftsmen who were already skilled in carving marble, making **mosaics** and building arches, domes, fountains, and towers. Sometimes, they took columns and stones from ruined buildings and recycled them to make new ones. Often buildings were very plain outside and brilliantly decorated inside, with walls, domes, and ceilings covered with brightly colored tiles or wonderfully carved plaster.

Mosques

The most important building for any Muslim was the mosque. It was used not only for prayer and preaching but also as a place for public meetings, teaching, and studying. The basic requirements of a mosque were simple—a shady hall for prayer and a pool or fountain for washing before going to pray. Most mosques also had a **minaret** from which a **muezzin** could call people to come for prayers.

Public Buildings

Large Muslim cities were protected by huge walls. Inside, they usually had a covered bazaar and an open market for shopping, public bathhouses, and often a hospital and a college. Sometimes they also had a fortified citadel where the people could hide in case of attack.

Palaces and Gardens

Muslim rulers lived in splendid palaces, which were usually surrounded by flower-filled gardens full of fountains and pools. For a desert people, a leafy garden and the sound of running water was like a vision of heaven. Our word "paradise" comes from the Persian for "a walled garden." At Samarra in Iraq, a 3-mile strip of palaces and gardens ran for 20 miles along a river bank and included two tracks for horse races, a hunting park, and a mosque big enough for an entire army to pray in all at once. The caliph Al-Mu'tasim, who started the building in 836, called it "He Who Sees It, Rejoices." The most famous surviving palaces are the Alhambra at Granada in Spain and the Topkapi in Istanbul. Both are now museums which attract thousands of tourists each year.

The strong walls and elegant pavilions of the Alhambra in Granada, last stronghold of Islam in Spain.

Sinan's masterpiece, the Selimye mosque at Edirne (Adrianople), built in 1569–1575.

SINAN

Sinan (1489–1588) lived to be almost 100 years old and built or rebuilt more buildings than any known architect in the history of the world—over 300, including 79 mosques, 34 palaces, 33 baths, 55 schools, 19 tombs, 16 poorhouses, and 7 colleges.

Born the son of a Greek Christian mason, Sinan was drafted into the Ottoman army and became a military engineer, building bridges and forts. He only began working as an architect when he was 49 years old and never stopped working for the rest of his life.

SOURCE 10

The use of colour in architecture represents a special Islamic achievement, and one that strongly contrasts with Western buildings. Every weary traveler in Iran will have had the experience, on approaching a mud-colored town, of being cheered by the turquoise or blue tiles on the dome or conical roof of the tomb of a saint or of the local mosque.

*From The Man-Made Setting by Richard Ettinghausen, in **The World of Islam** (Bernard Lewis, ed.), 1976.*

The Art of War

In theory, the Islamic world was the Dar-ul-Islam—the House of Peace—and the rest of the world was the Dar-ul-Kufr—the Land of Disbelief. In practice, there was often as much fighting within the Islamic world as along its frontiers.

Raids and Sieges

The usual style of fighting among desert Arabs was the razzia, a surprise raid on another tribe, usually to capture its horses, camels, or other livestock. During the course of their conquests, the Arabs had to learn new styles of warfare—how to organize big armies for full-scale battles, how to lay siege to cities with strong walls, and how to fight at sea in ships. They also learned how to use new weapons, such as huge catapults for hurling rocks and naphtha, a chemical which set fire to things.

Soldiers in Power

Rulers were expected to be warriors. Often their coins show them carrying a sword or mounted on horseback. Many rulers protected themselves with bodyguards of thousands of picked men. Often these were Mamluks— Turkish slaves from Central Asia. Their generals often held the real power. Mamluks ruled Egypt and Syria from 1250 to 1517. Other Turkish ex-soldiers were to rule kingdoms as far apart as Algiers in North Africa, Yemen in Arabia, and Bengal in India.

*A 9th century Muslim/15th century Christian **Mamluk**, handbook of warfare, showing soldiers using missiles with inflammable heads filled with naphtha.*

A Military Machine

The Ottomans created one of the most powerful armies ever known. From the 15th century to the 17th century it seemed almost unbeatable. The core of this army were the **Janissaries**. Suleiman the Magnificent raised their number to 12,000. They were recruited as boys from the Christian provinces of Greece and the Balkans. They were converted to Islam and toughened up by working on farms before being trained to fight. They were the sultan's slaves and completely loyal to him, having no families of their own. They also served as police and stopped riots.

The other parts of the army consisted of artillery and cavalry. Unlike the Janissaries, who were paid, fed, and equipped by the sultan, the cavalry fought in return for grants of land. All troops were also rewarded by the right to loot captured towns.

SOURCE 11

Spies must always go to all parts, disguised as merchants, holy men, medicine-sellers, or beggars, and report on all that they hear. For it has often happened that governors, officers, and commanders have plotted mutiny and rebellion against the king, but a spy came and informed him, so he at once set out, took them by surprise, and spoiled their plans.

*From **Rules for Kings** by Nizam Al-Mulk (1018–1092).*

SOURCE 12

They begin to shoot at 8 years of age and practice continuously for 10 or 12 years. The result is that their arms become extremely strong, and they become so expert that no object is too small for them to hit. The bows they use are not made of a single piece of wood but of sinews and ox horns fastened with glue and flax. They aim with such certainty that in battle they can pierce a man's eye. The distances which they shoot are almost incredible. By frequent practice they become able without any difficulty to hit their enemy unawares by shooting backwards as they ride away.

*From **Third Turkish Letter** by Ogier Ghiselin de Busbecq, 1560.*

THE SLAVE SULTAN

Baybars (1223–1277) was born a Turk, enslaved by Mongols, and sold to the Sultan of Egypt. He soon became one of the Sultan's bodyguards. In 1250 he captured Louis IX, the Crusader King of France. In 1260 he wiped out a Mongol army that had invaded Palestine. He hoped the Sultan would reward him with the town of Aleppo. When he did not, Baybars murdered him and became Sultan himself. As ruler he reunited Egypt and Syria and forced the Crusaders out of many of their castles and cities, such as Haifa and Antioch. He commanded 15 campaigns in person, winning victories in places as far apart as Libya, Turkey, and Persia. Generous, brave, religious, and a great builder, he died after swallowing a poisoned drink intended for someone else.

A Wider World

Bridges to the West: Spain and Sicily

Christian contact with Spain and Sicily when they were ruled by Muslims helped spread knowledge of such novelties as windmills, paper-making, **citrus** fruits, rice, cotton and sugarcane to Europe.

Spain was conquered by Muslim armies in just five years, between 711 and 716. In 756 Abdur-Rahman, the only Umayyad to escape alive when the Abbasids seized power in 750, arrived in Cordoba and set up an independent kingdom. His Umayyad successors made Spain strong and wealthy. But by the 11th century, the small Christian kingdoms surviving in the mountainous north had begun to counter-attack. By then, Muslim Spain was divided between 30 different little kingdoms, which were too weak in the end to prevent Christian reconquest. Toledo was taken by Christians in 1085, Cordoba in 1236, and, finally, mountain-ringed Granada in 1492.

New Ideas, New Things, New Words

Muslim rule left a lasting mark on the Spanish language. Hundreds of Spanish words come from Arabic and some have passed into English. Many of the words relate to trade, crops, war, crafts, buildings, music, and city life.

Arabic	Spanish	English
Amir ar-rahl	Almirante	Admiral
Habl	Cable	Cable
Laimun	Limon	Lemon
Mustaq	Mosquete	Musket
Naranj	Naranja	Orange
Qahwa	Cafe	Coffee
Qutun	Algodon	Cotton
Qitar	Gitarra	Guitar
Ruzz	Arroz	Rice
Sakk	Cheque	Cheque
Sukkar	Azucar	Sugar
Ta'rif	Tarifa	Tariff

Sicily

The Muslim conquest of Sicily began in 827 but was not complete until 966. By 1091 Sicily was back in Christian hands again. But Roger II (1105–1154) and Frederick II (1198–1250) continued have to Muslim scholars and advisers. Muslims established Europe's first medical colleges at Salerno and Palermo.

The Book of Roger

The Moroccan geographer Al-Idrisi spent 15 years compiling a map of the entire known world for Roger II of Sicily. Al-Idrisi studied all the best works of previous geographers and interviewed pilgrims, merchants, and sailors about the countries they had visited. Sicily, in the middle of the Mediterranean Sea, was an ideal base for this great project. The atlas was finally published as both a book, with maps, and as a solid silver disc 79 inches across and weighing over 330 pounds. Al-Idrisi knew that Britain was an island, but thought that it was winter there all year round.

ZIRYAB

Ziryab came to Cordoba from Baghdad in 822 and stayed in Spain until his death in 857. He was famous as a poet and singer, but he was also very influential as a trendsetter, bringing to the West the fashions, recipes, and hairstyles of Baghdad, Islam's biggest city. He was probably the first to suggest that the dishes in a meal should be served in a particular order. He favored using fine glassware at table, as well as gold and silver objects. He also set the style of wearing different kinds of clothing as the seasons changed.

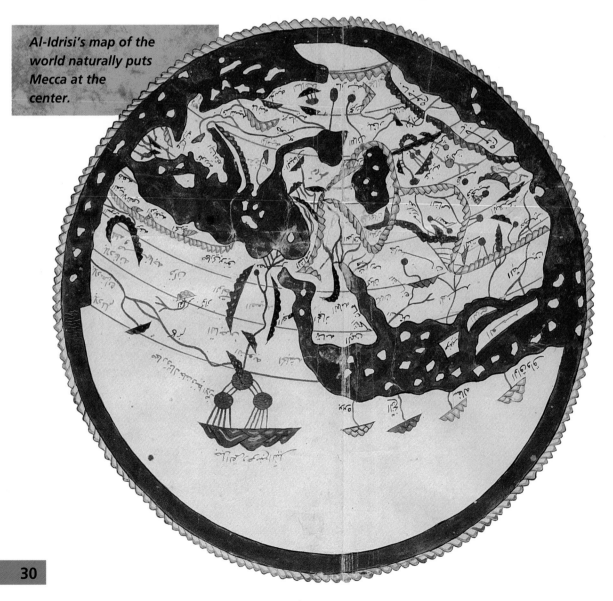

Al-Idrisi's map of the world naturally puts Mecca at the center.

Frontiers of Faith: Islam in Africa and Asia

Long after the Islamic conquests ended, the faith continued to spread beyond the former realm. It was carried by merchants, scholars, and holy men who often converted local rulers after serving them as advisers or doctors.

Africa

Traders sailing down the Red Sea to Zanzibar to buy **cloves** brought Islam to the coast of East Africa. In West Africa, the trade ran across the Sahara, exchanging fine horses, salt, and metal goods for gold and slaves. Arab visitors were, however, often shocked that forbidden customs continued alongside Islam—such as going naked or eating dogs. Islam is still winning many new converts in Africa today.

Asia

Islam spread into Asia across the Indian Ocean and along the Silk Road through the **steppes** to China. By 1200, there were communities of Muslim traders in Gujarat, on the northwest coast of India, and in Bengal, on the northeast. By 1300 Muslim communities were established along the coast of Burma and by 1500 on Sumatra and Java.

In China, the conquering Mongol Dynasty (1279–1368) brought in Muslims to serve as government officials. After the Dynasty fell, the Muslims remained in Kansu and Yunnan.

As in Africa, people who called themselves Muslims often continued with customs from their previous religions, especially when this involved fortunetelling or spells for warding off sickness or bad luck.

SOURCE 1

The Africans have some very good qualities. It is completely safe in their country. They are careful to say their prayers. On Fridays if a man does not get to the mosque early, he cannot find a corner to pray in on account of the crowd. Another of their good habits is wearing clean white clothes on Fridays. Yet another is their wish to learn the Qur'an by heart. They put their children in chains if they are slow to remember it.

*From **Travels** by Ibn Battuta, 1354.*

SOURCE 2

Throughout the area where Islam spread, the ruler was the chief merchant; he controlled all essential trade and traders. His most important official in dealing with foreigners was the Shabandar (Ruler of the Port) who by reason of his duties was in most cases a foreigner. Foreign Muslims tended to become Shabandars. They were able to indicate what was good form at the great Muslim courts abroad and to recommend the adoption of Islam as a means of extending the ruler's own power. They also introduced Muslim scholars and holy men to establish centers for Islamic **propaganda**. The courts became centers of Islamic learning.

*From **A History of Southeast Asia** by D. G. E. Hall, 1954.*

LEO AFRICANUS

Al-Hasan Al-Wazzan (1485–1554) was born in Granada, Spain, but brought up in Fez, Morocco. In 1510 he went with his father across the Sahara to Muslim West Africa and saw the great city of Timbuktu. In 1518 he went on a mission to Sultan Selim I in Istanbul. On his way back, he was captured by Christians who were so impressed by him that they sent him to Pope Leo, who baptized him with his own name as "Leo the African"—Leo Africanus. Africanus learned Italian and Latin and wrote a *Description of Africa* based on his travels. For 300 years this remained Europe's most important source of information about Africa. Somehow Africanus was able to return to his North African home and died a Muslim.

Endless Journey: The Travels of Ibn Battuta

Ibn Battuta spent almost 30 years traveling nearly 75,000 miles throughout the Islamic world.

Ibn Battuta (1304–1369) was brought up in Tangier, Morocco, and trained to be a judge. In 1325 at the age 21, he set out to make the pilgrimage to Mecca and to study with famous teachers in Egypt and Syria. By the time he got to Egypt he decided to see as much of the world as possible. He was one of the first people ever to travel just out of curiosity.

Pilgrims traveling together for safety from robbers.

The Traveler

After visiting Syria and Mecca, Ibn Battuta went east as far as Azerbaijan, then south to Yemen and East Africa, then back via Oman and the Persian Gulf to reach Mecca again in 1332. From there he went north to Turkey, across the Black Sea to southern Russia, and, after a round trip to Byzantium, through Central Asia into India.

By the time he got to India, Ibn Battuta's travels had already made him famous. The ruler of India made him chief judge of Delhi, then sent him on a mission to China. On the way he was robbed and then shipwrecked, losing all the gifts he was taking to the Emperor of China.

Map showing travels of Ibn Battuta.

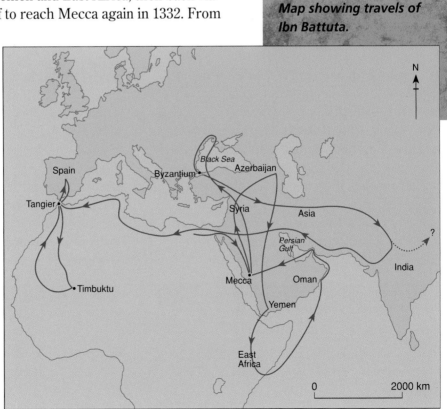

Spain · Byzantium · Black Sea · Azerbaijan · Tangier · Syria · Asia · Persian Gulf · India · Timbuktu · Mecca · Oman · Yemen · East Africa · N · 0 · 2000 km · ?

The Refugee

Afraid to go back to Delhi, Ibn Battuta fled to the remote Maldive Islands, where he again worked as a judge for two years and got married. Unfortunately the people of the Maldives thought him too strict as a judge, so he went on to Sri Lanka, was shipwrecked again, got mixed up in a war, and made a trip to Bengal. Finally he decided to try again to get to China.

The Diplomat

Ibn Battuta sailed to Sumatra, where the local Muslim ruler gave him a ship of his own. According to Ibn Battuta, he then sailed to China, visited the court at Beijing and finally made his way back by sea to Iraq. His account of China and Chinese customs is quite accurate, but also rather short and muddled. It is possible that he never actually went there himself, but described what he learned from reading or from talking to other travelers.

The Writer

Ibn Battuta certainly was in Syria and Egypt when the plague known as the Black Death struck in 1348–1349. Returning to his homeland, Morocco, Ibn Battuta made two final expeditions—to Granada in Spain and across the Sahara to Mali in West Africa. Finally in 1353 he ended his wanderings and dictated his memoirs to a professional writer, Ibn Juzayy—who may have added in information from other travel books he had read.

SOURCE 4

The people of the Maldive Islands are honest and religious. Their bodies are weak, they are unused to fighting, and their armor is prayer. Once when I ordered a thief's hand to be cut off, a number of those in the room fainted.

*From **Travels** by Ibn Battuta, 1354.*

SOURCE 3

No one is allowed to pass into Syria without a passport from Egypt, nor into Egypt without a passport from Syria as a precaution against spies. The responsibility of guarding the road has been given to a Bedouin tribe. Each night they smooth the sand of tracks, then in the morning the governor comes to examine it. If he finds any track on it, he commands the Bedouins to bring whoever made it, and they set out in pursuit and never fail to catch him.

*From **Travels** by Ibn Battuta, 1354.*

SOURCE 5

The Chinese themselves are unbelievers, who worship idols and burn their dead like Hindus. In every Chinese city there is a district for Muslims in which they live by themselves and in which they have mosques. The Muslims are honored and respected. The Chinese unbelievers eat the flesh of pigs and dogs and sell it in their markets.

*From **Travels** by Ibn Battuta, 1354.*

Rival Realms

The Rise of the Ottomans

Followers of a frontier fighter called Osman created an Islamic realm, which lasted longer than any other—six centuries.

Osman was the leader of a small band of Muslim frontier warriors. His men fought for land and honor, and by doing so enlarged the territories of Islam. In 1326 his son, Orhan, captured the important city of Bursa, which became the first capital of a growing Ottoman state. Later, Ottomans conquered European lands, thus gradually surrounding a shrinking Byzantine Empire. Three times they tried to take Constantinople, the capital of Byzantium and gateway between Europe and Asia. Three times they failed.

SOURCE 1

A young man, warlike, inspiring fear rather than respect, laughing rarely, keen for knowledge, generous, stubborn, bold in all things, and eager for fame. Every day he has history books read to him. Nothing gives him more pleasure than to study the state of the world and the science of war. The Empire of the World, he says, must be one— one faith and one kingdom. To make this unity there is no place in the world more worthy than Constantinople.

This is a description of Mehmet II by Giacomo Langusto, an Italian who met Mehmet II around 1450. Quoted in Istanbul and the Civilization of the Ottoman Empire by Bernard Lewis, 1963.

The Fall of Constantinople

Mehmet II (reigned 1451–1581) was only 23 years old when he became Sultan, but he was determined to take Constantinople and so end the Christian empire of Byzantium for good. The siege involved the biggest artillery bombardment in the history of warfare to that date—1453. There were 8,000 defenders against 20 times as many attackers. The last Byzantine emperor died fighting in the streets, and with him died a realm over 1,000 years old. Mehmet II was truly entitled to call himself "the Conqueror."

The Rise of Istanbul

At the time of its capture, Constantinople was a run-down shadow of the great city it had once been. The population had fallen to about 50,000. Mehmet II ordered that people should be sent from all over his realm to repopulate his new capital, which was renamed Istanbul. By 1480 the population was up to 70,000; by 1550, it was about 500,000, more than 40 percent of whom were Christian or Jewish.

Mehmet II converted the huge cathedral of Hagia Sophia ("Holy Wisdom") into a mosque and began a program of building new mosques and palaces, which was continued by his successors and their officials. The mosque that Mehmet had built incorporated soup-kitchens, baths, a hostel for travelers and a leather market. Topkapi Serai, the Sultan's chief palace, became so vast that the kitchens alone employed 1,000 people. Free public baths were a major feature of the city. The large ones were surrounded by stables, cook-shops, coffeehouses and booths selling towels, slippers, and fruit drinks.

SOURCE 2

SULEIMAN THE MAGNIFICENT

To avoid the dangers of disputed successions, the Ottomans adopted the "law of **fratricide**". The principle underlying this was that it was better for a few men to die, than that the world should be thrown into disorder. On the succession of each new sultan, his surviving brothers were strangled with a silken bowstring, a form of execution reserved for those whose blood it was forbidden to shed. European visitors spoke with horror of this law which did, however, preserve the Ottoman Realm from the dynastic quarrels that were causing so much trouble elsewhere.

From **Istanbul and the Civilization of the Ottoman Empire** by Bernard Lewis, 1963.

Suleiman (1499–1566) was the greatest of all the Ottoman sultans. His subjects called him "the Lawgiver", because his busy government sent out so many orders. Europeans called him "Magnificent" because his court was so splendid. He spent much of his life at war, capturing the cities of Belgrade, Tripoli, and Aden and the island of Rhodes, and conquering Hungary and Iraq. But, he was also a great builder of mosques and schools and was famous for never being unjust to anyone.

Suleiman the Magnificent rides through piles of dead enemies at the Battle of Mohacs in Hungary in 1526. Notice the artist's concern to show artillery and the Janissaries with their high headdresses. Painted by Nakkas Osman in 1588.

Government, Army, and Realm

The Ottoman realm was organized for war and continued to expand until 1699.

The Ottomans developed a new way of recruiting soldiers and officials called **devshirme** (assembly). Officers were sent out to the Balkans to choose the fittest young Christians they could find. They were converted to Islam and trained to serve the sultan as his slaves. Ninety percent were hired out to farmers to toughen them up and learn Turkish, before being trained for the army's crack unit—the Janissaries. The cleverest 10 percent were sent to the sultan's palace for a crash course in languages, mathematics, and good manners. After four years the very best became junior officials, and the rest were sent to the cavalry.

Who Held the Power?

For 10 generations the Ottomans were led by able and hard-working sultans. But after the death of Suleiman the Magnificent in 1566, the sultans who followed him were lazy and pleasure-loving rulers who preferred to stay in their palaces rather than leading their army in person. Their wives, viziers, and generals made the key decisions. Corruption became common at court and there were riots in the cities and banditry in the countryside. When Sultan Osman II (1618–1622) tried to reform the army he was murdered by his own bodyguards.

The Grand Vizier (Chief Minister) chairs a meeting of the Sultan's council of advisers.

Assault on Vienna

Every spring the Ottoman army set out for a frontier to conquer more territory. In 1529 an army of 250,000 raided deep into Germany and tried to capture Vienna. But the army retreated when winter set in and food became scarce. By 1541, the Ottomans had conquered most of Hungary. By 1600, however, the realm had become so large that the army could scarcely get to the frontier, fight, and get back to Istanbul within the summer campaigning season. In 1683 an Ottoman army made one last effort to take Vienna. Thanks to a rescue-force led by the Polish King, John Sobieski, the Ottomans were utterly defeated. In 1699 for the first time, they signed a treaty that gave up territory. The realm had begun to shrink.

KOCHU BEY

Kochu Bey was born a Christian and was rounded up as part of the devshirme. He rose to become a close adviser to Murad IV (reigned 1623–1640) who tried to reform the realm. At Murad's request, Kochu Bey wrote a report about what was going wrong. He blamed sultans for not ruling in person and appointing their best friends as ministers instead of choosing the best person. The result was plotting, corruption, and waste, leading to ever heavier taxes, which crushed the poor. All of this was basically true, but nothing much was done about it.

SOURCE 3

The Sultan himself appoints all men to their duties, and in doing so pays no attention to wealth or rank but only considers merit. Those who hold the highest posts are very often the sons of shepherds and herdsmen and, so far from being ashamed of their birth, they make it a subject of boasting— the less they owe to their forefathers and the accident of birth, the greater is the pride they feel. Thus among the Turks, honor and power are the rewards of ability; those who are dishonest and slothful never rise to the top.

*From **First Turkish Letter** by Ogier Ghiselin de Busbecq, 1555.*

SOURCE 4

When the enemy is near and a battle is expected, the armor is brought out, but it consists mostly of old pieces picked up from battlefields. You can imagine how badly it fits its wearers. One man's breast-plate is too small, another's helmet is too large, another's coat of mail is too heavy. There is something wrong everywhere; but they bear it calmly and think that only a coward finds fault with his arms, and they swear to do well in the fight, whatever their equipment may be. Such is the confidence which comes from repeated victories and constant experience of war.

*From **Third Turkish Letter** by Ogier Ghiselin de Busbecq, 1560.*

Shahs and Shi'ites

After centuries of being weak and divided, Iran was revived as a great power in the 1500s.

The Safavid Dynasty, who came to rule Iran, began as leaders of a religious brotherhood of Shi'ite Muslims. The discipline and loyalty of its members made it easy to turn into an army. In 1501 the 14-year-old Ismail Safavi declared himself Shah (King) of Iran, and by 1510 had conquered the whole country. Iran was converted from a Sunni country into the only Shi'ite one in the Islamic world—which it still is.

Shah Ismail at the Battle of Chaldiran in 1514. It was said that he could cut a man from the shoulders to the saddle in a single stroke.

SOURCE 5

The king, Shah Abbas is sturdy and healthy. He has extraordinary strength and with his sword can cut a man in two at a single blow. In his food he is simple, as also in his dress, and this is to set an example to his subjects. He is very strict in executing justice. From this it comes about that in his country there are so very few murderers and robbers. He has to be obeyed without question; anyone failing in the slightest will pay for it with his head.

This source is from a report by Father Simon to the Pope in 1604.

MUHAMMAD IBN HUSAYN BAHA AD-DIN AL-AMILI

Muhammad Ibn Husayn Baha ad-Din Al-Amili (1546–1622) was the wonder of his age—an expert at almost everything. Born in Syria, he was educated in religion, mathematics, and medicine. He made his way to Isfahan, where Shah Abbas made him chief judge. He wrote excellent poetry and stories, a book about astronomy, and a textbook of arithmetic. He also helped Abbas design the layout of Isfahan.

An Age of Greatness

Safavid power was at its height under Shah Abbas the Great, who ruled for over 40 years (1587–1629). He built up a powerful army with 500 cannons and 6,000 muskets. In 1598, he decided to move his capital from the western frontier city of Tabriz to Isfahan, in the heart of his territory. Under the wise and strong rule of Abbas, Isfahan became a great center of learning, art, and industry, famed for its paintings, silks, and carpets. With a population of more than 1 million, Isfahan had 273 public baths, 162 mosques, 48 colleges, and an immense bazaar covering 12 square miles.

A Long Decline

After the death of Abbas, Iran was weakened by bad rulers, too weak or too lazy to keep the army strong and defend the country from its neighbors. By the 1700s much of Isfahan had been destroyed, and the country had fallen into chaos.

The Rise of the Moghuls

Moghul conquerors united most of India and created some of its greatest monuments.

Babur (1483–1530) was a descendant of the Mongols and was determined, like them, to win a realm by the sword. By the time he was 30 years old he had a small kingdom based on Kabul in Afghanistan. In 1526 he invaded India and, thanks to the Turkish gunners in his army, wiped out a much larger Indian force at Panipat. By 1529 he was master of northern India but died before he could really organize his new country.

Babur's son, Humayun (1508–1556), was driven out of India by one of his own generals. Thanks to Persian help, Humayun was finally able to regain power in 1555—only to break his neck soon after, falling down his library steps.

A Realm Enlarged

Humayun's son, Akbar (1542–1605), was only 13 years old when he became ruler, but he soon proved to be brave and able. He once killed a tiger single-handedly with only a sword. Leading his armies in person, he gained new lands in every direction, doubling the size of the Moghul realm. To show his tolerance of different religions, he married a Hindu princess, appointed Hindu bodyguards, and forbade Muslims to kill and eat cows because they were sacred to Hindus. By the time of his death, Akbar was ruling a population of 100 million people.

Moghul Achievements

The Moghul emperors delighted in music, poetry, dancing, and painting. Akbar had a library of 24,000 books illustrated with exquisite paintings—although he could not actually read. The Moghuls also built splendid mosques, palaces, forts, and gardens, including the most famous building in the world—the Taj Mahal, a tomb for the favorite wife of Emperor Shah Jahan. It took 20,000 men over 20 years to build. Its cost would have paid an entire army for two years.

SOURCE 6

India is a land of few charms. Its people are not good-looking. There are no good horses, dogs, grapes, melons, or fruits, no ice or cold water, no good bread or cooked food in the bazaars, no hot baths, no colleges. The good things about India are that it is a large country and has loads of gold and silver. Another good thing is that there are immense numbers of craftsmen for every kind of work.

*From **Memoirs** by Babur, in approximately 1530.*

SOURCE 7

He (Akbar) gave orders for the building in Agra—which by position is the center of India—of a grand fortress. The foundations were dug through seven layers of earth. The breadth of the wall was 10 feet and its height 197 feet. Every day 3,000 to 4,000 laborers carried on the work. This wonderful fortress was completed in the space of eight years.

*From **The Reign of Akbar** by Abul Fazl Ibn Mubarak, 1596.*

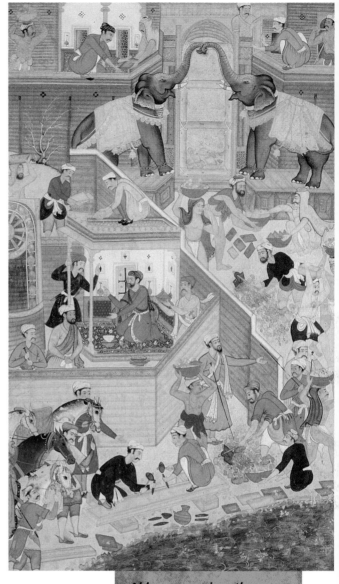

Akbar supervises the building of a new Moghul capital at Fatehpur Sikri. It was abandoned after just 14 years, because the water supply was inadequate.

ABUL FAZL IBN MUBARAK

Abul Fazl Ibn Mubarak (1550–1602) was one of Akbar's closest friends. Unlike most of Akbar's officials, who were Persians, Afghans, Turks, or other types of foreigners, Abul Fazl was actually an Indian. But like all members of the ruling class, including Akbar himself, Abul Fazl spoke and wrote in Persian, the language of government and literature. Abul Fazl is mainly remembered as the author of two important books—a history of Akbar's reign and a description of his realm.

Islam Past and Present

Muslims believe that they number more than 1 billion people. The number of Muslims continues to increase, both by birth and **conversion**, especially in Africa.

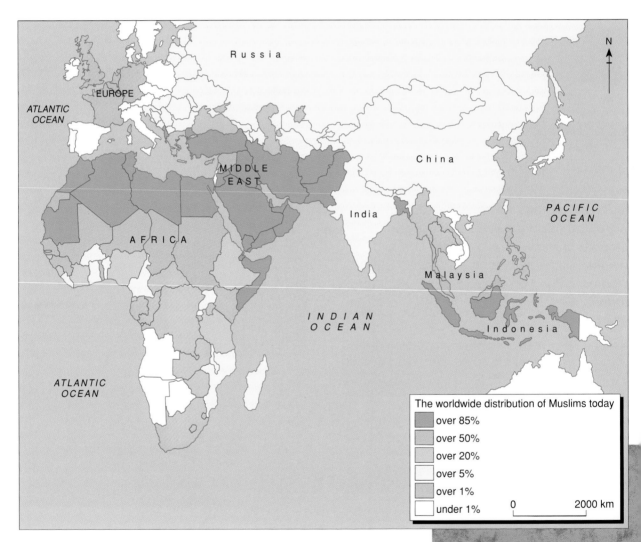

The worldwide distribution of Muslims today

- over 85%
- over 50%
- over 20%
- over 5%
- over 1%
- under 1%

0   2000 km

This map shows the main countries that have large Muslim populations today.

The Rival Realms: Decline and Fall

During the 1500s, control of artillery enabled the Ottomans to build up the largest ever Islamic realm, while the Moghuls and Safavids did the same in India and Iran. At that time they were far more powerful than any European state. With a population of 50 million, the Ottoman realm had more than 10 times more people than Britain in the 1500s. But, the rival realms lost their power by fighting each other and failing to keep up with the inventions which made European countries increasingly wealthy and powerful—such as the printing-press, steam-powered machinery, iron ships, and railroads.

By the 1800s most of the Islamic world was under some sort of Western control. Even the great Ottoman realm had lost most of its territory, although it did not finally collapse until it backed the losing side in World War I.

Revival and Renewal

During the present century, the countries of the Islamic world have regained their independence. The discovery of oil in many Arab countries, Iran, and Indonesia has given their governments wealth and power. Better health care and diets have led to rapid population growth. Throughout the Muslim world people hope for a better life for themselves and their children.

Majorities and Minorities

Muslims account for a majority of the population in about 50 countries. Most of these are in the Middle East, Africa, Central Asia, and Southeast Asia. The most **populous** are Indonesia, Pakistan, Bangladesh, Turkey, Iran, and Egypt.

Almost 100 million Muslims live in India and about 50 million in China, where they are both minority populations. There are Muslim minorities of tens of millions in Nigeria and the Philippines. Muslims also make up the largest religious minority in such European countries as Britain, France, and Germany.

SOURCE 1

Every year as the world grows smaller the Muslim countries are drawn closer together. Their number includes some of the world's wealthiest as well as poorest populations. Yet in the Qur'an they share a doctrine which lays particular stress on social justice.

*From **Islam in the World** by Malise Ruthven, 1984.*

Back to the Future?

When Muslim countries got back their independence from the countries that conquered them, their new governments usually tried to rule and develop them by using the methods of Western or Communist countries. This often led to a situation in which a few got the power and wealth, while the masses stayed poor and powerless. Many Muslims have come to see Islam as the best way forward because it is neither Western nor Communist but rooted in their own past.

This picture shows Muslim pilgrims standing on the plain of Arafat outside Mecca at the climax of the Hajj. For one day a year it becomes a city of 2 million people—the largest single human assembly in the world.

Time Line

570	Birth of Muhammad.
622	Hijra—Muhammad and the Muslims move to Medina.
630	Muslims capture Mecca.
632	Death of Muhammad.
636	Muslim armies decisively defeat Byzantines at Battle of Yarmuk.
656	Death of Uthman ends rule by Rashidun ("rightly-guided Caliphs").
661	Death of Ali, son-in-law of Muhammad.
711–716	Muslim conquest of Spain.
717	Muslim armies fail to capture Constantinople.
750	Umayyad Dynasty replaced by Abbasids.
758–762	Building of Baghdad.
836	Building of Samarra begins
969	Foundation of Cairo.
1071	Seljuq Turks decisively defeat a Byzantine army at Manzikert.
1085	Toledo, Spain, returns to Christian rule.
1095	Pope Urban II proclaims the First Crusade.
1099	Crusaders capture Jerusalem.
1250	Mamluk rule established in Egypt.
1258	Sack of Baghdad by the Mongols.
1260	Mamluks decisively defeat Mongols at Ayn Jalut in Palestine.
1291	Muslims recapture the port of Acre (Akka) ending Crusader rule.
1326	Ottomans establish their capital at Bursa.
1348–1349	Black Death devastates the Islamic world.
1453	Ottomans capture Constantinople.
1492	Fall of Granada ends Muslim rule in Spain.
1501	Ismail Safavi proclaims himself Shah of Persia.
1510	Safavid takeover of Persia complete.
1514	Ottomans defeat Safavids at Battle of Chalderan.
1517	Ottoman's conquest ends Mamluk rule of Egypt.
1526	Moghuls begin conquest of India with decisive victory at Battle of Panipat.
1529	Ottomans decisively defeat Hungarian army at Battle of Mohacs but fail to capture Vienna.
1571	Ottoman navy defeated at Battle of Lepanto, curbing their naval power in the Mediterranean.
1598	Safavid capital moves from Tabriz to Isfahan.
1605	Death of Moghul Emperor Akbar.
1683	Ottomans fail to capture Vienna.
1699	Treaty of Karlowitz—Ottomans give up territory for the first time.

Glossary

alchemy A false science, based on the belief that chemistry could be a form of magic.

aristocrats People born into a privileged, and usually powerful class.

astrolabe Instrument used for measuring the position of stars.

astrology Study of the stars and planets with a view to foretelling events.

astronomy The scientific study of the stars and planets.

bazaar Permanent marketplace, usually covered.

citadel Fortified strongpoint, usually on a hill above the residential part of a city.

citrus Group of fruits including orange, lemon and grapefruit.

cloves Dried flowerbud of a tropical tree, used as a strong spice in cooking.

convert To persuade someone to believe in a different religion.

devshirme Round-up of Christian boys recruited to serve the Ottoman sultan.

dhimmi protected religious groups under Islam, such as Christians and Jews.

dynasty Ruling family.

fratricide Murder of a brother.

Hajj The pilgrimage to Mecca.

hijra The emigration of Muhammad and his followers from Mecca to Medina.

idol An image of a god, usually made of stone or metal or wood.

intolerant Not willing to put up with different points of view.

irrigation Methods of bringing water to dry fields.

Janissary Literally "new troops", elite infantry corps of the Ottoman army.

Judaism The Jewish religion.

liberator Someone who sets other people free.

Mamluk Slave soldier.

minaret A slender tower on a mosque, from which the call to prayer is sounded.

mosaic Picture made up of tiny pieces of colored tile.

muezzin Mosque official who calls people to prayer.

muhtasib Market inspector who enforces hygiene and fair trading rules.

nomad Person who lives a wandering life in search of pasture for flocks.

oasis Well-watered area in a desert.

papyrus Kind of reed which was beaten flat to make a writing material.

parchment Very thin scraped animal skin used for writing on.

persecute Torment someone, usually on account of his or her beliefs.

populous Having a large population.

propaganda Messages intended to persuade people to a particular point of view.

prophet Teacher inspired by God.

Qur'an Literally "recitation', the Holy Book of Islam.

Rashidun The first four "rightly-guided" Caliphs.

revelation Important knowledge uncovered in a message from God.

Salat Daily prayers.

Saum Fasting, going without food or drink.

scripture Holy writings.

Shadahah Statement of basic Muslim beliefs.

souk Covered market, often shaped like a long tunnel.

steppes Flat, dry, wind-swept plains of Central Asia.

Sufi Muslim who tries to get close to God, often by chanting or dancing.

superstition False belief about religion.

synagogue Jewish place for worship.

tolerant To put up with and be fair to people whose ways or opinions are different from your own.

Torah First five books of the Old Testament, constituting the core of the Jewish scriptures.

Ulama Judges learned in Islamic law.

vizier High-ranking minister serving a sultan.

Zakat Charity tax.

Index